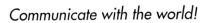

Language is Music

Over 70 Fun & Easy Tips to Learn Foreign Languages

Communicate with the world!

Susanna Zaraysky

Kaleidomundi

Dedication

To my parents Rimma and Isak Zaraysky for forcing me to take piano and clarinet lessons, even though I didn't want to practice every day. It was also very wise that you snuck me into French class in the 7th grade. (My 6th grade teacher didn't think I was ready for foreign languages and signed a document stating that I should not be allowed to take a foreign language in the 7th grade. My parents changed her answer on the form before submitting it to my new school. We can all laugh now at my 6th grade teacher's poor judgement of my potential!)

Dr. Oliver Sacks, if it weren't for your illuminating article, "Stereo Sue" in the New Yorker magazine, and your book, Musicophilia, I may have never solved my linguistic mystery and this book may have never been written.

Advance Praise for *Language is Music*

"I love it! I think it will help people who want to learn, and those who are curious about additional language learning. Many people want to learn a language but are frightened, or disappointed by the courses they have taken. Reading *Language is Music* will encourage them to try again, on their own and with friendly supporters."

- Dr. Elba Maldonado-Colon, Professor
Department of Elementary Education Bilingual Program,
San Jose State University

"LET IT JUST ROLL OFF YOUR TONGUE!
With lyrical insight and solid experience, Susanna Zaraysky, author of *Language is Music*, provides easy steps for learning a language. Gone are the boring, disconnected strategies that most of us remember from school. You've never learned a language this quickly and easily. Zaraysky's methods embody fun, connection, rhythm, and above all...music."

- Suzanne Lettrick, M.Ed
Educator and Founder of The Global Education and Action Network

"Forget dictionaries and phrase books . . . Susanna Zaraysky's easy-to-use guide to language learning is indispensable for any serious language learner wanting to become fluent--not just conversationally proficient--in another language. *Language is Music* will teach you how to make language acquisition a part of your daily life, and to recreate the kind of total-immersion environment necessary for fluency. Highly recommended reading for aspiring polyglots. Pick up this book and you too will be all ears!"

- Justin Liang, speaks Japanese, Mandarin, Cantonese, Marshallese, and intermediate Spanish

"Back in France, I spent many years learning "academic" English in school. But I progressed much faster when I forced myself to listen to the BBC or not look at the subtitles when watching an American movie. I wish I had Susanna's book with me then. It's full of creative ideas and practical tips that are indispensable complements to the traditional methods of learning foreign languages -- and it's coming from someone you can trust, she speaks so many of them!"

  - Philippe Levy, French native speaker

"This book is great. It showed me a new approach to learning a language. I will put the book to good use. As a foreign English speaker, I spent many years at school learning English and did not make much progress. I learned a lot of the tips that I read in this book with time. However if I had read this book earlier, it would have made my life much easier and I would have saved so much time. I am going to apply the tips in *Language is Music* into learning a third language: Spanish. This time, I am sure I will make huge progress much faster. Not only is *Language is Music* useful in acquiring a foreign language, but the resources and websites in the book are valuable for someone who wants to travel abroad."

  - Fabien Hsu, French native speaker

"*Language Is Music* is a unique tool for language learners. The great amount of insights are matched only by the thorough list of on-line and off-line language learning resources. From the first page, you can feel Susanna's joyful and refreshing attitude to the world. She is having a lot of fun dealing with the Tower of Babel and she makes it possible for her readership to have fun too. Her travel experiences and love for languages are the paradigm of how anyone can become a citizen of the world."

  - Carmelo Fontana, Co-founder of an incubating online language learning education company

Language is Music
Over 70 Fun & Easy Tips to Learn Foreign Languages Fast
Part of the *Create Your World* book series
Copyright © 2009 by Susanna Zaraysky.

Second Edition

Kaleidomundi
PO Box 1253
Cupertino, CA 95015
USA
www.createyourworldbooks.com
Email: info@kaleidomundi.com

ISBN: 978-0-9820189-9-6
LCCN: 2008910798

Cover and Interior Design by Krista Thomas
Edited by Frank Reuter and Britt Breu
Typefaces used in this book are credited as follows: Futura, designed by Paul Renner; and Baskerville, designed by John Baskerville.

Create Your World Book Series

Mission

- To create global citizens who are engaged in the world, passionate about world events and confident international travelers and communicators.
- To empower you to interact and appreciate other cultures and ways of life.
- To give you the skills to travel economically and see the world.
- To teach you how to easily learn foreign languages and have fun.

Be your own peacemaker!
Be your own ambassador!
Create your world!

Books In This Series

Travel Happy, Budget Low
Over 200 Money Saving Tips to See the World

Language is Music
Over 70 Fun & Easy Tips to Learn Foreign Languages

Benefits of this Book

Have fun and advance your foreign language capabilities.
Listen to music and the radio, watch TV, attend cultural events, talk to people and enjoy the language learning process. You don't have to stare all day at verb conjugation charts and get nightmares of your language teacher beating you with a stick because of pronunciation mistakes.

Cost effective language learning. The free and low cost tips as well as over 90 Internet resources enable to you speak a language without spending a ton of money on plane tickets, tutors and intensive language programs. You don't have to leave the country or even leave your home.

Learn faster than from the traditional "memorize and regurgitate" lessons used in schools and universities.

The language becomes part of your daily life. The new language is alive and not just a list of vocabulary words.

Created by a self-made expert. Without expensive tutors or intensive language classes abroad, I learned these techniques naturally.

Table Of Contents

Why Should I Learn a Foreign Language?

We've all heard the word "globalization." The phenomenon has various effects in our lives. One of them is the necessity to be able to communicate with people in different parts of the world. As traveling, working, immigrating, and living abroad become more common, increasing numbers of people are multilingual. Government jobs pay a bonus for each foreign language an employee can speak.

Even if you don't engage in international business, being multilingual is important.

According to United States Census data, 20% of US households speak a language other than English. Politicians and companies are targeting their messages to non-English-speaking communities. One of the 2008 Democratic Presidential Primary debates was telecast in Spanish. In the 2006 California Democratic Gubernatorial Race, the candidates' Chinese speaking family members made campaign announcements in Mandarin.

The reality is we have to be multilingual to thrive in this globalized economy. Young generations see the necessity to learn foreign languages for their careers.

I got my first job out of college because I spoke Russian. The local division of the Department of Commerce's Export Assistance Program was going to help host a summit between United States Vice President Al Gore and the Russian Prime Minister Victor Chernomyrdin in Silicon Valley. The office needed a Russian speaker to help the Russian VIPs attending the summit. I had to get a special security clearance to participate. Not only was I the Russian speaking guide, I also listened to presentations by the CEOs of major Silicon Valley companies. I was only 21 years old. Without my Russian knowledge, the doors to this high-powered summit meeting would have been closed.

A few months later, my Spanish skills were in demand. The Argentine Secretary of Communication was visiting Silicon Valley on a trade visit, and I was the only completely fluent Spanish speaker in our office. Even though I wasn't even old enough to legally rent a car, my boss convinced the car rental company to let me drive the Argentine Secretary of Commerce and his entourage around in a rented van! Like with the Russian delegation, I attended meetings with top Silicon Valley executives whom I would otherwise not have had the opportunity to meet. Being in an Argentine environment was wonderful practice for me because I was going to Argentina the following year as a Rotary Ambassadorial Scholar.

Neither of these opportunities would have been available to me if I didn't speak Russian or Spanish.

Imagine foreign languages are like keys, both in the musical and physical sense. The more keys your voice can produce equals more physical keys you have to open doors to new horizons. Let me open up your world to the sounds of other languages. It will open doors you never knew existed!

Myths and Current Foreign Language Education

MYTH: To learn a foreign language, you have to live in the country where the foreign language is spoken.

REALITY: No. I learned Spanish and Italian fluently without living in a Spanish speaking country or Italy. Plus, I had almost perfect accents in both languages. If the myth were true, then all the immigrants and refugees living in the United States would speak perfect English. Many of them don't and it's because foreign language instruction is focused on grammar and memorization. Students get bored and frustrated with this traditional approach. They don't learn how to appreciate the rhythm and flow of the language, nor see that it can be fun and easy to learn.

MYTH: If you can't go to the country where it is spoken, you need to work one-on-one with a tutor to learn the language.

REALITY: I am living proof that you don't need a private tutor. With the exception of a few private lessons in Bosnia, I never had a tutor.

MYTH: To get a good accent, you have to spend a long time in a country where the language is spoken.

REALITY: If that were true, then Arnold Schwarzenneger, the Austrian-born movie star and current governor of California, would be able to pronounce the word "California" like a native speaker and not with a heavy German accent.

According to the International Institute of Education, the number of American students studying abroad has increased 250% since the 1990s. Other statistics show that more and more people are studying languages, but they are using the same ineffective methods that have failed millions of students in the past. Americans study languages, but we are known internationally for being abysmal foreign language speakers. Why? Because we simply memorize vocabulary lists to "learn" words. BORING! Lists of words are just useless stockpiles if not used creatively and naturally. It's like taking a cooking class and making a recipe without tasting the food after cooking it, or reading a car operating manual without riding in the car and feeling and seeing how it runs. We have to feel, taste, and breathe a language to learn.

The *Language is Music* book aims to remedy our horrible foreign language learning process. You will realize you have the power to learn languages successfully in my fun and engaging way, without having to take expensive classes or leave the country.

Introduction

This book is a supplement to traditional forms of language education and is meant to make language learning alive and fun. It's not a replacement for grammar lessons, classes, and educational materials. You still have to learn grammar to know the structure of the language you are learning. Just like musicians have to know chords, timing, and other music fundamentals, you need the same for languages. Though I have learned a great deal by listening to foreign languages being spoken by native speakers, I needed to understand and know grammar and language structure to properly reproduce and create correct sentences in those languages. My teachers' explanations and grammar books were essential.

Why I wrote this book

Language is a window to the world. Without being able to communicate, my world would be bland and colorless. Having worked and traveled in former war zones, I have seen that much of the violence and tension in the world could be reduced with improved communication and global understanding, but people either lack the desire for dialogue or simply cannot understand each other.

Having labored through many dull language classes, I saw how ineffective rote memorization techniques alienated and discouraged students. I knew I could change language education to make it more fun and engaging. In Taiwan, I saw a teacher stare into a book, just reading English phrases in a monotone voice and asking her students to repeat. She didn't notice her students were looking out the window and were bored out of their minds. After normal school, Taiwanese kids went to cram schools to memorize even more information and take extra English lessons, but they were scared to death to speak to a native English speaker. After years of memorizing dictionaries, like they did to learn thousands of Chinese characters, most Taiwanese adolescents needed glasses. Since I was born with eye problems, I had no desire to weaken my own or other people's eyes while pursuing the study of foreign languages. I knew it was possible to learn without major eye strain.

While reading Dr. Oliver Sacks' book *Musicophilia*, about the neurological aspects of music, I became inspired to write about how music helped me learn foreign languages. (This was the second time in less than two years that Dr. Sacks' writing provoked a profound and life altering change in my life. You'll read more about this as I describe the mystery he helped me solve about my ability to learn foreign languages.)

After solving my personal mystery about why I was so dexterous in learning foreign languages, I developed fun tricks and lessons to enable others to be successful. Creating this book was a way for me to contribute to international communication and to teach people they can be their own interpreters and peacemakers.

My mystery

Of the 10 languages I have studied, I speak English, Russian, Spanish, French, and Italian fluently and Serbo-Croatian and Portuguese at an intermediate level.

I used to speak basic Hungarian when I lived in Budapest in the fall of 1997, but I have lost most of it. I can still read some Hebrew, but I can't speak. Two weeks into my Arabic class, my Arabic language instruction CDs broke my stereo and I couldn't play them anymore. Unfortunately, I only remember a few words in Arabic and can barely read.

People always asked me how I was able to learn so many languages without taking intensive language classes abroad, or having private tutors. Languages came easily and I didn't understand why other people struggled so much. Although memorizing grammatical structures and vocabulary charts in middle school, high school, and college was not enjoyable, I seemed to be one of the minority of foreign language learners who actually learned grammar quite well using traditional instructional methods. Grammar was like a mathematical formula which I simply learned and applied when needed. Since I was good at math, language structure was not a terribly difficult framework to learn. However, I saw that many of my other fellow students failed miserably with grammar. They thought they could never learn a foreign language.

Seeing my own father struggle to learn English, despite living in the United States for 28 years, made me realize that traditional foreign language education was not effective. Something I was attuned to helped me learn foreign languages more readily than methods used in school. But I didn't know what it was.

I couldn't understand why people who spoke one Romance language (French, Spanish, Italian, Portuguese, or Romanian) as their native language would have so much trouble learning another Romance language. I thought learning another Latin-based language should be really easy for them because the languages had similar structures and many cognates. But it wasn't. I was stumped.

It was not just my navigation of grammar and language structure that amazed people, it was my accent and ability to copy sounds perfectly or almost perfectly. I could just say a few words in a foreign language and people would automatically tell me how good I was in their language, even before I produced any complex sentences or used sophisticated vocabulary. In fact, even when I did make some small mistakes with grammar, people still said I spoke impeccably. My accent and excellent pronunciation almost deafened native speakers to my mistakes.

I knew I had a gift, but I did not know what to do with it or how to convey the technique other people. I was a mystery to myself.

My friends, when introducing me, would say: *This is Susanna, she speaks seven languages. She's the walking Tower of Babel.*

I would cringe, give my friends the evil eye, and pretend I was all right with their cheerful, but annoying introduction. Later on in private, I would ask them NEVER to introduce me like that again. I hated being associated with my rare skill. Does a car mechanic want to go to a party and discuss the differences between a Mercedes and a Honda engine? I doubt it. Talking about motor oil doesn't mix well with cocktails. The mechanic is at the party to socialize and not talk about work. No matter how adamant I was about not talking about my polyglot skills, people always repeated this embarrassing introduction.

I hated it because I would always draw the same comments: *You must be really smart. How did you learn all those languages? Did you live in all those countries? How can you afford to travel so much? I've been trying to learn Spanish for years. What methods do you recommend? Should I move to Costa Rica for the summer and take Spanish lessons?*

When I told the inquirers to just take a Spanish class, listen to Spanish language radio, watch Spanish language television stations, and go to a Latino part of town to do their shopping, they couldn't believe it was that easy. But language learning was easy—for me.

But what about all those subjunctive verbs and weird past tense formations?

I simply replied: Learn them, memorize the verb conjugations charts. Spanish is easy compared to other languages.

They would stare in amazement.

My frustration

What more could I tell them? I grew up with two languages, Russian and English.

I heard some Spanish while growing up in California. This helped me when I formally studied the language when I was 16.

I was a sponge that absorbed sounds easily. If someone couldn't roll an "r" or make a soft "n" sound, I assumed they had a hearing problem. I couldn't reformat other peoples' ears.

Say 'hi' for me. I want to hear what X language sounds like, casual acquaintances would say.

Did I look like a clown for hire? Was my hair that frizzy and were my clothes that colorful that I looked like a circus act?

Even when I wasn't presented as "the multilingual one," my truth would always manifest itself somehow. If I heard someone speaking French at a party, I would speak to them in French. At the end of a night, I might have spoken in five different languages in a social setting. Eyes would always pop when people heard me switch tongues and speak with little or no accent. I wasn't showing off, I was just communicating. It was totally natural to me. But to them, it was like an opera singer serenading with a different aria every thirty minutes. What was I supposed to do? Hide my languages and pretend not to understand people? I tried that, but I wasn't good enough of an actress to conceal my true nature.

My life was a rainbow with various linguistic colors. Dreams transpired with a myriad of words, some even from languages I didn't speak fluently. In my conscious life, various intonations, accents, semantic structures, and alphabets were always floating in my mind at the same time. No one language or accent embodied me and I could tell that I changed personalities depending on what language I was speaking. I was a true chameleon, but not from chromatic changes of fur or skin color, but by language. The phonetic structures made me generate myself by making sounds in different parts of my mouth, throat, and nose, creating distinct physical sensations when I pouted my lips in French or rolled a super strong "r" in Russian. Even the sounds of the languages affected my relationship to what I was saying. The "singsongy" tenor of Brazilian Portuguese made it hard for me to take myself seriously when speaking with Brazilians.

Like a musical instrument, my body resonated to various frequencies. I was like a mini-orchestra played by just one person. On the brain level, semantic and grammatical rules governed how I constructed my thoughts. With the passive reflexive and noun-adjective agreements in French, I had to always be incredibly lucid when speaking the language to avert mispronouncing words and forming my sentences poorly. Whereas in Spanish, I felt like the frequent use of the passive voice made me less responsible because I spoke about events happening to me, rather than taking responsibility for my actions. With this mix of sounds and grammar in my head, I yearned to be able to communicate by switching between phonetic and semantic structures with grace.

When my friends were baffled because I prohibited them from showcasing my linguistic talents, I wasn't so much mad at them as I was frustrated with myself. My friends would tell me they were proud to have such a polyglot friend. "If I had your talent for languages, I would not want to hide it," they said.

What they didn't know was my "skill" and "gift" were often a major pain and psychological weight. Who would want to advertise their weaknesses? The more people knew of my abilities, the more requests I would get for translation and interpretation— my incarnation of hell. Sometimes, even scrubbing the toilet was more enjoyable than being the Tower of Babel tour guide. The worst was when the person I was interpreting for wasn't particularly bright or was asking stupid questions. I was embarrassed for being their spokesperson.

Nobody understood me.

People often told me I was wasting my time in my career choice of the year because I wasn't using my language skills to the maximum. I thought diplomacy would be my route.

Some of my friends seriously suggested I become a spy. *The CIA, FBI, and Interpol would love to have someone like you. They wouldn't even have to train you. You're a natural chameleon.* I was too silly to be a 21st century Mata Hari.

Many times I would be frustrated with all the questions about my language skills because I didn't want so much attention, and I became annoyed at hearing the same questions all the time. I realized I had to write down what I knew to help other people. But I still didn't know what was so special about the way I could quickly and easily learn languages.

Natural talent? No.

Was it the fact that I grew up speaking Russian at home and English outside of the home?

No. Though being bilingual may have made it slightly easier for me to learn other languages than for those who grew up monolingually, that wasn't the secret to my talent. I knew other people from immigrant backgrounds who spoke two languages and they had trouble learning foreign languages.

Was I a gifted musician with perfect pitch who could copy sounds?

No. I loved many different types of music and had been going to classical music concerts ever since I was a young child, but I was no virtuoso. I was a mediocre clarinet and piano player. Although I enjoyed singing, I sang off key more times than I cared to admit.

Was it genetic?

Even before my father lost some of his hearing, he was horrible with language. His mother used to say that an elephant had walked on his ears.

My maternal grandparents learned many languages in school

and my maternal grandmother was a German language and literature professor, but no one on my mother's side of the family was as good with accents and sounds as I was.

Discovery

At the age of 29, I found out that I only saw with one eye at a time. My world turned upside down.

I read Dr. Oliver Sacks' June 2006 *New Yorker* article, "Stereo Sue", about a woman who was born cross-eyed and developed three dimensional vision in her 40s through vision exercises. Prior to reading the article, I had no idea my being born cross-eyed made only see with one eye at a time. I thought my two eye surgeries made me see like everyone else. Even though both of my eyes worked, my brain only registered images from one eye at a time. With just two-dimensional vision, I had limited depth perception.

That article revolutionized my world. I was in shock for weeks as I tried to grasp what the world looked like for the 95% of the population who could see in depth. If my world was flat, what could most other people see that I couldn't?

Though extremely painful emotionally, this new information about my visual limitations solved my language mystery. I had unconsciously developed excellent hearing that had enabled me to learn foreign languages. As in many cases when someone is disabled with one of their senses, another part of the body over-compensates. My three-dimensional world consisted of my two ears and whichever eye my brain was registering.

Much of language acquisition comes from hearing. We do converse with our eyes, but mostly, communication is about being a good listener and paying attention to the way someone is speaking and what they are saying, especially with tone and inflections. My good hearing was making up for my partial visual disability and helping me pick up accents and recreate sounds. I realized I learned language like I would a piece of music. I copied what I heard.

How could I transform my solved mystery to a set of language learning guidelines to help other people?

Since I hated translating and interpreting, I had to share my gift with others and teach people how to communicate in other languages and be their own guides in the Tower of Babel. I was getting lonely being one of the few polyglots around! I wanted people to be able to communicate for themselves and not rely on interpreters. More than anything, I wanted international communication to be easier so people could solve problems and live peacefully.

I thought through tricks and methods I had used over the years to learn languages and saw that I had many tips to share. My advice does not require people to have a visual disability like I do—or to be an incredibly gifted musician. It just requires training your brain to absorb foreign languages like music. When stroke survivors lose their ability to speak, they listen to music to regain their speaking skills. Music is integral in learning to communicate.

After many years of not knowing what to do with my gift, I am bringing it to you. May you enjoy and learn to speak in another tongue. Your world will never be the same.

Listen and you will speak.

By the way, the name of my publishing company, Kaleidomundi, means (beautifully shaped world). The name Kaleidomundi derives from the Greek καλός (kalos for beautiful) + εἶδος (eidos for shapes) + **mundi** (plural form of the Latin word mundus for world).

Susanna Zaraysky
October 2008

Section 1: Conductor's Notes

Instructions on How to Think of
Language as Music

1. Tune your ears

Learning a new language means you have to change your key
and tune. Dancing the cha-cha to waltz music is like speaking a
new language while still using the rhythm of your mother tongue.
Let yourself take in the sounds of the language as though you
were listening to a new piece of music.

Even if you are just a beginner and barely know any words, you
can still learn by listening. Pay attention to how people speak.
Does it seem like they are reading a phone number or rattling of
a list of numbers? Are they angry? Happy? Sometimes, you have
to shut off your brain and inclination to interpret and analyze.
Listen to the words spoken to you and listen to your intuition.

Enjoy!

Language is music.

 Personal Story

*During my first days of my semester abroad in Budapest, Hungary in
1997, I was in the advisor's office waiting to speak to him. He was
on the phone talking in Hungarian. Even though I knew just a few
words in Hungarian, I could surmise he was telling the person on the
other line a phone number because of the melody of his sentence. The
way he pronounced the succession of numbers sounded dramatically
different from the rest of his conversation.*

2. Mozart to the rescue!
"You cannot reproduce a sound you cannot hear."
> - Alfred Tomatis, French ear specialist and founder of the
>   Tomatis method for language acquisition and speech therapy

Alfred Tomatis founded a therapy program to train ears to hear
sounds they didn't previously hear. Tomatis discovered that the

reason people have accents in other languages and have trouble replicating sounds is that they simply don't hear the sounds of the other language correctly. Their ears have grown accustomed to processing sounds from their mother tongue.

Have you ever wondered why the French have trouble with the word "the" in English? It's because English has many more high pitch sounds than French and the "th" sound doesn't exist in French. If people don't hear sounds of a particular frequency, they can't recreate them no matter how hard they try. Just like a saxophone can make sounds that the piano can't, languages have different registers and frequencies. Sometimes, people can't hear their own accents in a foreign language even though they may have a strong one.

Tomatis created a training program with an electronic ear that filtered new sounds to the ear in order to train ear muscles to react and process new sounds. He also encouraged his patients to listen to the music of Amadeus Mozart because the music has a wide range of low and high pitched frequencies. I have never gone through Tomatis therapy and can not vouch for it, but listening to Mozart can only help you train your ears to listen.

Whether or not you espouse Tomatis' theories, I suggest listening to classical music regularly, especially before language lessons and conversation practice, to calm your body and mind and sharpen your ears.

www.tomatis.com

3. Stick to the beat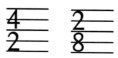

I hear this every time I take a dance lesson! Now, it's my turn to use it.

People learn basic music theory when they start piano or violin lessons. Some just pick up the guitar, learn some basic chords and notes, and then fumble around until they copy songs and melodies they already know. In either case, music students have to keep to the rhythm of the music. Waltzes are slow. The cha-cha is fast.

Would you drum to choral music?
Would you waltz to cha-cha music?
Would you play a 2/2 beat in 3/4 bar?

No. Every music has its beat. If you play a sonata as rap music, you may have a cacophonous succession of notes or a "creative" piece. In most cases, musicians stay loyal to the tempo of the music.

The same goes for language. The reason people have strong accents in other languages is because they are playing the music of the foreign language in the tempo and rhythm of their mother tongue. It's like dancing the waltz to cha-cha music.

If you listen to language as music and pay attention to the rhythm, flow, accentuation, and timing of the words, you are more likely to easily learn the language and have a good accent.

4. Read and listen between the lines

My voice teacher told me singing was not about the notes themselves, but about the distances and relationships between the notes. When listening to your target language, pay attention to the range of sounds in a given word or sentence. Are many of the sounds similar to each other? Do you like how soft vowels sound next to hard consonants? The French language has many words beginning and ending with vowels and some phrases can be hard to decipher for beginners. French speakers pronounce their multi-vowel words in a *legato* form, connecting all the vowel sounds. Can you figure out that there are two separate words in a phrase where one word ends in a vowel and another one begins with a vowel or does it sound like one long word?

5. Listen before creating

Would you start to play the violin before hearing what violin music sounds like? Most likely not. You need to get used to the musicality of a language before you imitate its sounds. Remember that as children we first learn to make sounds and then words. Babies and toddlers listen to language before they say their first words at the age of 1 or so. They hear first, then they speak. Not everyone in the world is literate, but almost everyone can speak at least one language.

6. Let's put the "la" in language

Starting to learn a language with grammar is like teaching a kid music theory before letting the child listen to songs and actually enjoy or get used to the melodies. BORING. A child wants to play a harmonica or sing along to a song and not learn about minor and major chords. Even as adults, we are lured by fun. Let's face it, who wants to start learning a language with grammar? Only someone who is a language afficionado or a linguist. Most of us learn to communicate. To talk, we need to pronounce words. We need to feel how the language sounds.

Think of speaking sentences in Japanese as singing a song. It's a lot more enjoyable than only concentrating on grammar and vocabulary. When you get frustrated with the language, remind yourself that it's just a game. Don't associate language learning with being scared, seeing your language teacher drilling you on verb conjugations in front of a dusty chalkboard. When US figure skater Sarah Hughes was the surprise gold medalist at the Salt Lake City Winter Olympics in 2002, journalists asked her how she won it despite all the stress and media attention. She said she was just having fun on the ice and didn't let herself cave into the pressure of winning. This is a great attitude to have to keep your cool. There will be times where you won't understand or will mispronounce things. Laugh it off. Learning can be enjoyable.

7. Length and melody

The length and melody of languages vary considerable and a foreign speaker has to literally get into the rhythm of the tongue to correctly create phrases. Some languages are very melodic, like Italian. Others are monotone. If you speak Japanese with an up and down Italian-style musicality, you will sound funny. When English speakers don't ride the waves of Italian and speak in flat or monotone sentences, they are missing out on the beauty of the Italian language.

Vietnamese speakers treat each syllable as a word. To an English speaker, Vietnamese may sound choppy. This explains why some Vietnamese sound like they are cutting off words when they speak in English. They are not used to pronouncing long words with multiple syllables. Those who speak languages with words consisting of more than one syllable have to change their pace of speaking and create fast short words in Vietnamese.

Arabic has long and short vowels. Pronouncing a word with a short vowel instead of a long vowel can completely change the meaning of the word. The same is true in music, if you hold a note longer than you should or play a staccato instead of a whole note, you are altering the music and may make the piece of music sound wrong.

8. Up and down

crescendo   *decrescendo*

Is there an upward pitch at the end of a sentence? Australians and people in California's Los Angeles and Orange Counties often end their sentences with a high note as though they are asking questions. Although it may sound like the speaker is not sure of him or herself, that is the way people in these areas speak English. This can be somewhat confusing for someone learning English who is not used to the accent. It may seem like the speaker is constantly asking questions.

9. Emphasis

fortissimo

Where is the emphasis in the word? Many times people mispronounce words in another language because they accent or emphasize the wrong part of the word. Hungarian, though extremely complicated grammatically, is easy to pronounce. The emphasis is always on the first syllable of the word. Always. Sentences in Hungarian always have a predictable sound. The emphasis will never be on the last syllable of the last word, as may happen in other languages when someone is trying to stress something in particular.

10. Fall in love

Romantic love is probably the easiest road to learning a foreign language. People learn fast when they want to communicate with a person with whom they are in love. If wedding bells are not driving you to learn, then you need to fall in love with the sounds of the language you are learning or something else about it that you like. If you don't like the language or how people speak it, it will be quite hard to force yourself to learn it well.

If you hate the sound of the language, but you have to learn it for work or another reason, look to identify with something endearing in the language or culture.

Personal Story

After living in Sarajevo, Bosnia designing economic development pro-

grams for 15 months, people asked me why I didn't speak the language fluently. They knew I was dexterous with languages and learned them quickly. As a native Russian speaker, Serbo-Croatian should have come easily to me because it is a Slavic language. However, I found the local speaking style to be too aggressive for my taste. I could speak at an intermediate level and I could communicate enough for my professional needs, but I was not motivated to become fluent.

11. Be calm

Your mind is like a sponge; it will absorb more when it is open and ready to take in information, not when it is contracted and stressed.

12. Muscle memory, Practice often

Athletes exercise often to train their muscles to act and react in specific ways. Musicians practice their chords many times before performing. Your voice and language ability work in similar ways. You can't take a language class twice a week, do your homework and then think you will learn the language. You have to practice often. Your vocal muscles need to practice making the sounds of your target language in order for it to come naturally.

13. Be tenacious and have patience.

You won't be a fluent speaker overnight. You have to develop the resolve to practice, forgive your mistakes and keep working. Be patient and kind to yourself, but keep your integrity about practicing the language. Soon, you will reap your rewards.

The Three Elements of Singing: Pronunciation (articulation), Phonation (tone), and Breathing

14. Appreciate the importance of good pronunciation

We articulate with our tongue and lips. Focus on how you move your mouth when making sounds. You may have to open your mouth more to better create sounds. Remember, singers have big mouths when they sing.

Some linguistic theorists explain that we have accents to mark our tribal affiliations to separate us from others. People like to speak to someone who sounds like them. It makes them feel comfortable. While light or medium accents in other languages are acceptable, if someone speaks with a heavy accent in another language, it can be very difficult for native speakers to understand them. Some native speakers may avoid communicating with people with bad accents because it sounds as though the language learner is butchering their language. In those cases, both the listener and speaker get frustrated. There are people who may write perfectly in another language and know grammar even better than native speakers of that language. However, if they have poor pronunciation, their grammatical knowledge will be practically useless in verbal communication. The ability to reproduce sounds correctly is vital for communication.

15. Tone

Tone is important in music and in language. Vietnamese and Mandarin are tonal languages, with words that sound similar, but are differentiated by having different tones. If you say something with the wrong tone, you may be saying something wrong or incomprehensible.

16. Breathing

Remember to stop and take a breath and exhale. You can be so excited to speak that all your words come out really fast with no breath in between words. The listener can't understand you and you are gasping for air.

Section 2: Listen, listen, listen

"All speech, written or spoken, is a
dead language, until it finds a willing
and prepared hearer."

-Robert Louis Stevenson,
Scottish author

17. Relax and listen to music in the language you are learning

Find music in your target language that you like. It doesn't matter if at first you don't understand the lyrics. Pick music you like. You may start singing along without even knowing what you are singing. That's fine. You are not only learning the rhythm of the language, you are learning new vocabulary.

Relax and close your eyes. Turn off the lights. Lay down or sit in a comfortable position. Close your eyes and listen to the music. Don't try to understand the words, just listen. You might fall asleep or day dream. Give yourself the time to simply listen and not do anything else. Your mind needs to be calm in order to absorb the sounds. Your ears need no other distractions to let them properly hear all the high, medium and low frequencies of the language. Do this regularly.

Your local library may have a foreign language CD selection. Large music stores carry foreign music sections and may let you listen to the music before buying.

You can find songs to download for a cost at:
www.itunes.com
www.rhapsody.com

Browse music videos in the language:
www.youtube.com

18. Listen to the music in the background

Turn on the music while driving, doing household chores, cooking, gardening, etc. Even if you are just passively listening to the music, the rhythms of the language will become more familiar to you. Exposure is key.

Personal Story

When I worked in post-war Sarajevo, I lived in an apartment that had no television. I always listened to the radio on my small stereo. Even though most of the music was techno-pop music or Bosnian folk music which I didn't care for, I listened to it anyway to hear the language. I took a few Serbo-Croatian language lessons, but I got bored and wasn't motivated to continue. Since I already spoke Russian, another Slavic language, the Serbo-Croatian language lessons were slow and boring. To the surprise of my landlords and Bosnian friends, I was able to hold conversations and understand the language at an intermediate level without much effort on my part. I credit this in large part to listening to music. While I was preparing food or cleaning my apartment, I was singing along to music. The rhythm of the language got into me. My native fluency in Russian was a big help in being able to understand the basics of Serbo-Croatian and to pick up its sounds. However, despite the common roots of the languages, they are not similar. Many words are different, and there are sounds that are particular to each tongue. The music on the Sarajevo radio stations helped me get on the local wavelength.

19. Write down the lyrics as you listen

Listen to music with the lights on, your eyes open and a pencil in hand. Write the lyrics of the songs while listening. You will have to pause the music and rewind or repeat many times to get the words down. Some words will be hard to write because they may be idioms or slang that you haven't learned yet, but just write as much as you can understand. Remember that songwriters sometimes employ rarely used words just to make the song rhyme. They often play word games and compose their lyrics with words that sound alike or may even be spelled the same way, but have different meanings. Don't be frustrated with obscure words. Compare the lyrics you noted with the original song and see how well you were able to understand the song. Some CDs come with the lyrics inside the CD case. If you don't have them, look for them online on lyrics websites.

Once you have your version of the lyrics and the original, you can see how much you were able to understand from listening to the song. Use your dictionary to translate the words you don't know.

www.lyrics.com
www.azlyrics.com
www.smartlyrics.com
www.elyricsworld.com
http://music.yahoo.com/lyrics

If you can't locate the lyrics on the lyrics websites, just type in the name of the song in quotes in a web search. For example, type "New York, New York" and "lyrics" in the search.

20. Recognize grammatical patterns and conjugations in the lyrics

By paying attention not only to the content of the songs, but also the structure of the sentences, you will begin to recognize grammatical patterns.

Is the song in the present tense, future tense, or the past tense? Is the singer speaking in the subjunctive? Irregular verb patterns are easier to understand when you can hear them in context.

If you don't recognize some of the conjugations, look up the root verb in a verb conjugation chart to figure out which tense the verb is in. Keep in mind that when irregular verbs are conjugated, they may not at all look like their root.

21. Make a vocabulary list with words from the songs

To visually reinforce what you are learning from listening to music, write vocabulary words from the songs you are learning on flash cards or pieces of paper. On one side, write the word in your language and then write the word in the other language on the opposite side. When you are waiting in line in the grocery store, you can pull out the flash cards and study your new words. If you study one song a week and reinforce your learning by practicing your vocabulary with flash cards, you will quickly learn new words and have fun along the way.

22. Imagine the lyrics in your head

If the song is a story, then close your eyes as you hear the music and think of what the songwriter is talking about. Create the story in your mind as you listen. You'll retain the words from the songs better than by just memorizing them from a vocabulary chart. You will be more apt to use the words when you need to communicate. For example, the famous *New York, New York* song speaks of someone coming to New York and seeing the city is alive, even at night. Imagine someone arriving in New York city, or another big city, and seeing the city full of bright lights and action. People are walking around, eating in restaurants, and drinking in cafes. The streets are full of cars and buses.

Do this type of a visualization exercise to make the music come alive for you. Utilize your imagination.

23. Draw pictures of the story

After imagining the story described in the song, draw the story. By utilizing your drawing skills, you will be fortifying the song in your mind. Visual reinforcement is important in making the words of the song be real to you.

24. Listen to the music in your head

When you hear songs in your head, you usually hear the music in its original form, without your accent. Relax, close your eyes, and play the song in your mind. Be your own stereo. You are letting your brain get used to the sounds of the language and recreating it in your mind before you try to sing it yourself. Singers hear the notes in their brains before they open their mouths and sing.

Section 3: Concert Time

Play Your Instrument

SPEAK!

25. You are your instrument. Tune it!

Your body is a musical instrument. It's not just your mouth that makes sounds. Your body vibrates in different places to different sounds. When you speak in your language, where is the sound coming from? Pay attention to that. The pharynx, oral cavity, and nasal cavity are the most important parts of the body that make sounds. However, the vibrations of the sounds make the chest, tracheal tree, and head areas resonate. Focus on the source of the sound and the resonance in your body. The more aware you are of your body, the better you will be at locating what parts of your body are activated when you speak.

When you speak in your new language, focus on what parts of your body are making the sounds. How does your mouth feel? Do you have to pout? Where does your tongue travel to make sounds? Look at yourself in the mirror when speaking in your native and target languages to notice differences. Does it feel different to speak in your target language than when you are speaking in your native tongue? If so, keep this in mind when you are speaking your target language. It's easy to slip back into your old habits of speaking. When you can tell that you are making sounds in your new language from the same part of the body where you speak your own language, correct yourself. Re-calibrate to the rhythm of the target language. This will help you develop a better accent. Remember, you are learning a new tone and you have to adjust your voice register to accommodate.

Some songs have many high notes, other are very low. Language is the same way. You have to listen to the musical nature of the language to feel how the words go up and down.

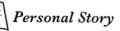 *Personal Story*

I can feel my nose vibrate when I make nasal vowel sounds in Portuguese. Russian is spoken in mostly melancholic minor keys that I produce in the mouth and deep throat areas. English rings to more joyful

major chords in my mouth and the back of my head. French has many guttural sounds that are not easy to reproduce for an English speaker, not used to using the back of the throat to speak. I find myself pouting when I speak in French to make its unique vowel sounds.

26. Don't be afraid to sound like Tarzan

Give up your ego. If you are a perfectionist, you need to take on an alter-ego of a fearless person who makes mistakes in your new language. In East Asian cultures, people often are hesitant to speak in a different language even if they have studied it because they are afraid of making mistakes. I noticed this when traveling in Taiwan and Japan. Don't worry. No one is perfect. You don't have to be.

Being intrepid may be part of your new soul. Face reality. You will make mistakes. You may occasionally make a fool out of yourself. Who cares? Native speakers know you are learning their language and will forgive your mistakes. In fact, once you can learn from your errors and laugh at yourself, you will feel much more relaxed. You won't learn to speak unless you give yourself the right to fail. You will learn from your mispronunciation and incorrect grammar. I had to be Tarzan before I could become multilingual. I wasn't born a polyglot. Like most infants, I cried when I was born!

27. Relax when speaking!

When people are uncomfortable in a new language, they often sound harsh or defensive when they speak, which makes native speakers uncomfortable. Keep this in mind when you are speaking. Even if you are struggling, try not to look very frustrated or mad, you may scare away people who would otherwise be patient and listen to you. Check your speaking style in a mirror.

28. Sing. Karaoke your way to fluency

Sing the songs you are listening to. Even if you are not ready to go on *American Idol*, sing to yourself in the shower. Your effort won't be embarrassing. Usually, your native accent will be diminished when you sing in another language. I am serious. I notice that people's accents sound much more native when they sing. If you memorize songs in a foreign language, you learn the cadence and melody of the language. Although you will most likely not serenade people as you have conversations in your new languages, knowing songs is a good ice-breaker when you are at parties and meet native speakers. Unless you are horribly out of tune, they will be impressed with your interest in learning about their culture and may help you learn even more melodies. Music moves the soul. You can move others with your mastery of their music. If you have a conversation partner (see **Section Seven**), you can practice your songs together.

29. Record yourself singing

Use a voice recorder (tape or digital) or use a recording program on your computer to record yourself singing the tunes. Compare your sound to the originals. This will help you hear how your melody compares to that of a native speaker. Continue listening to the original songs and you will see that the more you listen and practice singing, the closer you will sound to the original.

Section 4: Radio Time

Tune Into a New Frequency

30. Listen to a local radio station in the new language

Don't underestimate the power of the FM and AM bands on your radio dial. We may be in the Cyber age, but millions of people listen to the radio everyday for news, entertainment, and music. In the United States, where millions commute daily in cars, radio is a popular medium. Immigrant groups in the United States have many radio stations and broadcast in their native languages.

When you first start listening to radio broadcasts, the announcers may sound like they are emitting a stream or storm of sounds and not individual words. In time, you'll hear familiar words repeated and will learn to distinguish them. Language teachers call this "acquired competence." Like music, you can listen to the radio attentively and take notes, listen to it in the background or just close your eyes to listen without straining yourself to understand.

Personal Story

For years, I listened to Rádio Comercial Portuguesa, the Portuguese radio station in San José, California. The radio station served the Portuguese immigrant community from the Azores Islands. While driving and being stuck in traffic, I listened to their local advertisements for Portuguese companies that ranged from plumbing contractors and construction supply companies to Portuguese "padarias" (bakeries). I could care less about construction companies and their wonderful supplies, but I listened to the announcers just to get a feeling for the rhythm of Portuguese and to learn vocabulary. Since the community was very religious, the station broadcast their Catholic mass in Portuguese at the same time every day. I am not Catholic and was not keen on learning the "Our Father" prayer em portugues, but I listened anyway. The music was mostly not of my taste either. Old Portuguese fisherman songs and folk tunes dominated the programming. I loved melancholic fados, but they were rarely on air. It didn't matter. I was stuck in my car and had the choice of listening to news or music in English or learning more Portuguese. I chose the latter. The station often aired radio news directly from the national news service of Portugal, giving me news about many countries in the Portuguese speaking world.

The result was that, despite the fact that I had few opportunities to speak Portuguese, I was passively learning it for years. As a matter of fact, I thought that I spoke Portuguese like Tarzan because I had mostly taught myself the language and had only taken two basic classes in adult school. In 2006, while living in New York, my Brazilian roommate Carla invited Silvia, her friend from Brazil, to visit during Christmas. Silvia barely spoke English. I had to speak in Portuguese, even though I was embarrassed of what I thought was my Neanderthal-like command of the language. To my and everyone else's surprise, sophisticated words and long sentences came out of my mouth with ease. Carla and Silvia commented that my accent sounded like it was from Portugal. I found out that I knew much more Portuguese than I thought. All those years of listening to fishermen's songs and Catholic masses paid off. I spoke Portuguese! I had been reinforcing the vocabulary and sentence structure rules that I had learned by just listening to the radio. The music was inside of me for years.

You can create your own symphonies as well. Just listen!

(Now, my accent is more Brazilian sounding as I have traveled in Brazil, speaking to Brazilians.)

Turn the radio dial during different times of the day to look for radio stations. Some radio stations may not have 24-hour programming as they share the frequencies with other small radio stations.

Look in your phone book under the radio section. If you are in the US, use the Yellow Pages and look under "Radio Stations." The foreign language stations usually list their language in their title.

Go to the Yahoo Directory of radio stations **http://dir.yahoo.com/News_and_Media/ Radio/By_Region/** Look up the radio stations in your area, checking for the language you are learning. It's best to search under regions rather than your city. There might be a radio station in another city nearby that broadcasts in the language that you want. If you only look for radio stations in your town, you will not find others in your vicinity.

31. Listen to radio stations on the Internet

You can play radio stations on your computer while at work or at home. You can download programs and podcasts as MP3 files and keep them on your computer to listen to later or download to your MP3 player. Not only can you listen to radio programs made by immigrant groups in your area, you can listen to radio from around the world on the Internet. A wider variety of stations are available online than on your local radio dial.

Extra bonus: When you consume news from different parts of the world, you will gain a new perspective on current events and learn about places you may have never heard about. There are talk, music, news, political, sports and comedy shows and many other types of programming on the radio that can fit almost anyone's interests. Let's say you love to learn about cars. You can listen to car talk shows in another language. You may get new ideas for how to fix your own car and learn new words!

The following Google Directories list radio stations by language/ ethnic group, international broadcasting companies, and by region. Look for radio stations of interest in these directories. Try out a few and see which ones have programs that you like. Play the stations while you are working on your computer or just use them as background music.

By Language/Ethnic Group:
www.google.com/Top/Arts/Music/Styles/R/ Regional_and_Ethnic/

www.google.com/Top/Arts/Radio/ Regional/

www.worldtvradio.com/php/radio_channel_ language_lineup.php

By International Broadcasters:
www.google.com/Top/Arts/Radio/ International_Broadcasters/

Google Directories by Region:
www.google.com/Top/Regional/ Click the language and region you are interested in and look for the media section. (This is written in the language of the region.) For example, news and media in French is listed as "Actualité" and not "media"

By Country:
www.worldtvradio.com/php/radio_channel_ country_lineup.php

Section 5: Television for Homework

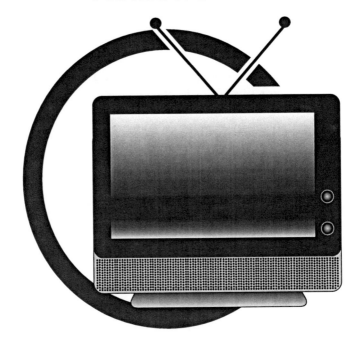

Watch TV, Learn to Speak

32. Watch television programs in the language

This may be the first time in your life when watching television is your homework. Take advantage of the opportunity!

Let's say you are learning Spanish. You have found a local Spanish language TV station in your area or you are watching the national Univision news. Even without knowing all the words, you will be able to get the gist of some of the news reports. The images and video footage of events already tell you what the news announcers are talking about. Tune into HOW they are speaking and the words they are using to describe the images on screen.

Even if you can't watch TV all the time, it's all right to do errands around the house as you listen to the TV in the background. Think of the TV as background music like you would hear in a café or restaurant. Even though it's not at the forefront of your consciousness, your brain is still processing it and getting used to the flow of the language. Remember, we listen before we speak.

Extra bonus: Not only will you be learning how the language sounds, you will also be exposed to news you may not see on your local or national television news. If you are learning Mandarin Chinese and find a local television news station broadcasting in your area, you may learn a great deal about the Chinese community that you never saw reported in mainstream news. You will learn about what is going on in places where the language is spoken. It's quite possible the Italian news will have more news about other European countries than a news channel in the United States or Taiwan. So, keep your mind open. You are not only learning a language, but another view of the world.

Check your local television listings for foreign language programs or stations. If you have cable or satellite TV, you should have more foreign language options.

33. Record, replay and write

Record the foreign language programs you are watching on TV. Replay the shows and listen closely to the content. Sit down and write down what the people are saying. Use a dictionary if necessary. You may have to rerun a show 20 times before you understand what the announcers or actors are saying. It doesn't matter how many times you have to repeat it. The more you hear the phrases, the easier it will be for you to grasp what is being said. Musicians often practice certain measures of songs over and over again until they get them right. They'll repeatedly listen to music recordings so that they can learn another musician's technique. Think of yourself as a nascent musician. You might be frustrated at first, but it will pay off later on when you understand TV scenes or news announcers without having to rewind and replay so many times.

34. Watch TV via the Internet

With so many television stations providing free live streaming content on the Internet, you don't have to pay for a heavy satellite to put on your balcony to hear Arabic from Al Jazeera. You can do it online. Many sites will let you see content for free.

To find television programs from different countries on the Internet:

By Language:
**www.worldtvradio.com/php/
TV_channel_language_lineup.php**

By Country:
**http://dir.yahoo.com/News_and_Media/
Television/By_Region/Countries**

**www.worldtvradio.com/php/TV_channel_
country_lineup.php**

www.wwitv.com

By Region:
http://dir.yahoo.com/News_and_Media/
Television/www.google.com/Top/Arts/
Television/Regional/

Section 6: Films to Fluency

Learn from the Stars!

Before television and the Internet, people learned about other countries and cultures through the motion picture industry. Foreign films show you how people communicate and act in other countries. You can learn idioms, mannerisms, gestures, cultural nuances, and other elements of culture and tradition that you can never truly pick up from a textbook. More sophisticated films may play word games and have subtle political messages that you may not understand as a beginning language student. Try to stay with simple and popular movies when you are just starting out.

35. Find the original version of movies in your target language

NEVER WATCH MOVIES DUBBED IN YOUR LANGUAGE!!!

Watching dubbed movies is a cardinal sin when it comes to learning languages. You lose most of the cultural experience when you watch a dubbed movie.

Living in Europe, I wondered why the Scandinavians and Dutch had such good accents in English, while the French, Spanish, and Italians were known for their heavy signature accents. Northern Europeans start learning English earlier than the French, Spanish, and Italians. But it's not only their early start that gives the Northern Europeans their wonderful pronunciation. Their teachers are not native English speakers. So, they are most likely not acquiring their stellar accents from just their instructors.

The Scandinavians watch many English language television programs and movies in their cinemas, as do the Mediterraneans. However, the Northern Europeans leave the soundtrack in the original language and just add subtitles in their respective tongues. The French, Spanish and Italians see English language actors speak in unnatural dubbed voices in their national languages. They are learning English in isolation from the sounds of native speakers. Learning a language in a vacuum is tough. You can let the world into your home by watching the original versions of movies, listening to how people really speak. Stay away from dubbed movies and TV programs!

A movie that is mostly conversation and no movement may be hard to follow. (The philosophical French movies fall into this category.) Action-packed *Indiana Jones* is much easier to understand than *Hiroshima Mon Amour* with the long scenes of just two people talking. Comedies may have a lot of jokes that will be hard to understand. Humor does not often translate well!

You can rent foreign movies at your local library. Look for cultural organizations in your neighborhood. They might have their own libraries with films from their native countries.

These two sites have a wide selection of international movies:
Netflix: **www.netflix.com**
Blockbuster: **www.blockbuster.com**

If you want to just watch certain scenes from movies, you can look for them on You Tube. Just type in the name of the movie and some words pertaining to the scene you want to see:
www.youtube.com

36. Watch international media with subtitles in multiple languages

The use of subtitles while watching TV and movies, especially authentic programming, is extremely useful in improving your language abilities. ViiKii is a website run by volunteers which features original TV programs and movies from all over the world and adds subtitles in a multitude of languages. Users can choose which languages they would like to see videos in, add subtitles as well as captions in the original language, as well as participate in culture and language discussions about the program. Use of ViiKii is free.

www.viikii.net

37. Watch and enjoy!

If you have a DVD player, go to the Menu options, turn on the subtitles in your language, and leave the audio in the original language. Relax, sit back, and just watch the movie and enjoy. Listen to the inflections in peoples' voices and how they communicate. Even if you can't keep up with the subtitles as you are concentrating on the conversations and actions, that's fine. The most important point is to focus on how the people are speaking, gesticulating, and acting. You can always rewind and watch the scenes over again.

38. Happy? Sad? Flirting?

Pay attention to how people sound as they express emotion. Can you tell from the sound of their voice how they feel? Does their voice sound light when they are giddy? How do they flirt? What may seem to you in your own language as anger may be a normal way of communicating in the other language. Just as music conveys emotion by speed, minor and major tones, and the heaviness or lightness of the sounds, so do our ways of speaking. Not only do you need to learn the words to express your feelings in your target language, but you also need to know how to convey your message with the sound and rhythm of your phrases. Native speakers will more easily comprehend your message if your words and tune are in harmony. If you are happy about something, but you are speaking in a tone that sounds angry to them, they won't necessarily know you are excited. They may think you are upset with them. Misunderstandings arise not just from words, but also through delivery.

 Personal Story

Be careful of how your linguistic background may program you to judge the tone of other languages. When hearing French speakers, I often think they are complaining because of their facial gestures and tone. Though the French are not shy in expressing their dissatisfaction, I have often misinterpreted their normal manner of speaking to be one of constant lament.

39. Watch movies in the original language without subtitles

Ignore the subtitles. Focus on the actions and the sound of the language. If you have a DVD player, go to your menu options and turn off the subtitles. If you are using a VCR, then cover up the subtitles with a piece of paper or tape at the bottom of your television screen and watch the movie without the subtitles. See how much of the movie you can understand by listening to the words, by paying attention to context and images, and by "turning off" your reading mind. Use your intuition to understand unknown words. Listen even if you don't understand!

Important words will be repeated throughout the movie. If the movie is about a train crash, you will hear words relating to trains, passengers, conductors, and rail tracks over and over again. The more you hear them, the more apt you will be to retain the words. When we are novices and know few words, we think we can't understand. While we are definitely unable to maintain a conversation or understand complicated phrases, we can still learn from non-verbal cues like glances, gestures, eye movement, crossed hands, and the like. Keep listening and maintain alert eyes to pick up on visual clues to what people are saying. Are they standing far from each other? Crossing their hands? Looking at their shoes instead of at the person in front of them? Think of what their body language is communicating.

40. Watch the movies without subtitles, then study the script

When you've trained yourself to watch the movies without translation and you are able to follow the actions and conversations to understand at least some of what is going on, read the script to get the full story. There are different ways to go about this. Read a scene first, translate the words you don't understand, and then watch the scene. Or you can do it in reverse. Watch the scene without subtitles, write down what you think the meaning of the conversations and actions are, and then read the script and look up the words and phrases you don't know.

See next page for website resources.

Scripts for non-English language movies:
http://simplyscripts.com/non_english_scripts.html

Websites with movie scripts for English language movies:
www.iscriptdb.com
www.sfy.ru
http://simplyscripts.com/movie.html
www.script-o-rama.com/snazzy/dircut.html
www.screenplays-online.de
www.movie-page.com/movie_scripts.htm

If you can't find the movie you are looking for on these websites, type the name of the movie you are looking for and the word for the "screenplay" or "movie script" in language of the movie into your web browser. For example, if you are looking for the screenplay for a French movie, it will be easier to find it on a French search engine like www.google.fr or www.yahoo.fr than an English language one. Type the name of the movie you desire and the French word for screenplay, scénario.

41. Listen, don't watch

Play the movie scene on your television with your eyes closed. Relax and listen to the words. When you don't have the video images to show you what is going on in the movie, you will have to focus in what is being said and how people speak. This is a good exercise in listening comprehension. Again, you will most likely have to rewind several times. Listen to the scenes several times and write down what you understand.

If you are at your computer, you can also listen to audio clips from movies on these websites:
wavcentral.com/movies.htm
www.moviesounds.com
www.wavcentral.com

Personal Story

When I taught English to professional adults in Argentina, the language school for which I worked gave me audio cassettes with scenes from two American movies, "As Good As It Gets" and "When Harry Met Sally." I don't know if the language school obtained the audio cassettes through legal means or not.

I sat with my students and listened to scenes from these movies. I tested them on how much they understood. I realized how hard it was to comprehend Billy Crystal's fast mumbles in "When Harry Met Sally." We had to rewind the scenes many times for my students to understand the context of the conversations. The exercise was important in improving their listening comprehension without visual cues.

42. Listen, watch, write

Watch the scenes *without* the subtitles. When you have both the audio and visual inputs, you will understand more of the conversations. As in the previous exercise, write down what you additionally understand when you are watching the scenes without subtitles and are becoming familiar with the conversation.

43. Listen, watch, read, write

View the scenes again *with* subtitles. Is there something that you didn't understand completely when you just listened to the movie or when you watched it without subtitles? Compare your comprehension of the scenes with the subtitles to what you understood when you just listened to the movie and when you watched the movie without subtitles. You can measure your listening comprehension progress with this exercise. If you do this regularly with various movie scenes, you will understand more and more of just the audio and you will not have to watch the movie with or without subtitles as many times to understand the dialogues.

44. Flash cards

As with the music lyrics, you have to visually reinforce whatever you learn from listening and watching. Write your new vocabulary words from the movies you are watching on flash cards or pieces of paper. On one side, write the word in your language and then write the word in the other language on the opposite side. When you are waiting in line somewhere or riding in public transportation, pull out the flash cards and study your new words. Studying your vocabulary with flash cards will help you to quickly learn new words and have fun along the way.

Section 7: Be Part of the Symphony

Speak with Others in Your
Target Language

45. Conversation exchange in person

Once you get used to the sound of your new language, you need to practice it and speak to a native speaker. Do a language exchange. Meet with a native speaker of the language you are studying who wants to speak and practice your language. Usually, you spend half the time speaking in your language and half the time in the other person's language. It's good to meet in person for a one-to-one conversation on a regular basis. You can meet for an hour a week and speak for 30 minutes in your language and half an hour in the other person's language or you can alternate days.

By meeting in person, you'll learn about the other person's culture and cuisine. Cook your native foods for each other or give a cooking lesson. Make it fun! Meeting a native person is the best way to learn body language and non-verbal cues. Communicating in a different language is not just about the words we speak, but also the unspoken body language of gestures, facial expressions, posture, and the physical distance one keeps between him or herself and the person with whom he/she is speaking. I've done language exchanges for several languages and it's been a great way to speak with a native speaker, learn idioms and slang, and have someone to correct my grammar and pronunciation.

If you live near a university, contact the international student office to ask how you can find a native speaker and do a language exchange. Many campuses have a bulletin board where you can post a sign for language exchange. They may also have a website where you can do the same thing.

When I was a student, I found Spanish and Italian language partners through the YWCA in Berkeley, California. Through a national program called English in Action, the YWCA was looking for volunteers to help foreign students and visiting scholars improve their English.

I asked the YWCA staff to help me find Spanish and Italian language exchange partners and they were happy to do so. Check with your local YWCA or YMCA to see if they offer language exchange services.
www.ymca.org
www.ywca.org

If there are immigrant or refugee groups in your area that speak the language you want to learn, contact the immigrant and refugee resettlement agency (like the International Rescue Committee or Catholic Charities) and ask if you can post a sign in their lobby for a language exchange partner. If the immigrant or refugee groups live in a particular part of town, go there and post flyers for language exchange in the libraries, laundry mats, cafés, or other places the community frequents. If you meet with someone who has recently arrived to your country, remember that they may be living on a small budget and may be in trauma. Don't organize meetings in restaurants they may not be able to afford. They may feel uncomfortable. Meet at their homes, in a park, or at the library.
www.theirc.org/where
www.catholiccharitiesusa.org

Look for cultural centers in your neighborhood that represent the language you are learning. The staff or volunteers there may be able to help you find someone with whom to practice the language. Locate a cultural organization in your area that represents the language you are learning. Call the nearest consulate or embassy of the country whose language you are learning and inquire about cultural centers in your area. The website of the embassy or consulate may even have links to cultural and language resources. Here's a website with a listing of all of the world's embassies:
www.embassyworld.com

Craigslist: Find the Craigslist page for your geographical area. In the Community section, there is a listing for activity partners. You can browse the postings for people searching for language exchange partners or post your own request.
www.craigslist.org

Conversation Exchange: You can locate a conversation partner in your area on this site.
www.conversationexchange.com

46. Look for interest groups or activities in your area

If you are a student, worker, immigrant, refugee, or visitor already living in a foreign country and you want to improve your skills in the national language, you should meet with native speakers. Do you like to play soccer, dance, watch movies, embroider, arrange flowers, hike, or have some other hobby? Look for community groups and activities that would interest you so you can meet local people who have similar interests. It's a great way to meet new people and make friends. You can also volunteer in the community.

Go to the Craigslist Community Section, where there are listings for events, activities, volunteers, ride share, activity partners, groups, musicians, politics, artists, and other categories. Browse through these sections to look for people, events, and groups that interest you.
www.craigslist.org

Find social and activity groups on Meet Up on Meet In in your geographical area. Type in your state and zip code and see what kind of groups exist in your area. If there isn't one that interests you, then just start one and organize an event.
www.meetup.com
www.meetin.org

47. Conversation exchange via the Internet

In addition to your language partner in your neighborhood, you can have a language buddy online. If you live in a remote area or a place that doesn't have foreigners or immigrants who speak your language of choice, you can still practice with a real native speaker for free on the Internet. At first, it may be difficult to understand the other person because of sound quality issues and the absence of body language. Remember to speak slowly and clearly. If the other person is speaking too fast, ask them to slow down. The services below are mostly free websites where you can find a language exchange partner with whom you can communicate by text, voice, or video chat. Many of the sites have language learning forums where you can interact with people from your language group who are learning the same foreign language. You can help each other in your learning process. Some of the sites have online tutorials and free downloads of educational materials.

www.mylanguageexchange.com
www.sharedtalk.com.
www.xlingo.com
www.conversationexchange.com
www.ringuage.com (For a fee.)
www.babbley.com (For Chinese and English.)
www.lingozone.com
www.language-buddy.com
www.livemocha.com
www.language-exchanges.org This is also called Mixer. Speak to your language buddy online via Skype (Voice Internet Protocol system that allows you to speak for free with other Skype users).
www.eslbase.com/language-exchange
www.friendsabroad.com
www.polyglot-learn-language.com
www.penpalnet.com
www.slf.ruhr-uni-bochum.de
www.italki.com
www.speakmania.com
www.huitalk.com

48. Cultural events

Before you buy a ticket to go abroad, you can experience foreign cultures, languages, and food nearby. You don't have to go to Mexico to learn about the Day of the Dead celebrations. Join a *fiesta* near your home.

The language you are studying will come alive at cultural events. You will not only hear native speakers talking, but you will have the opportunity to interact with people and practice your skills. Usually, people are open to helping language students who are attempting to learn their language. They may be quite flattered by your interest in their culture and language.

If you are studying an Asian language, keep in mind that many East Asian cultures celebrate Lunar New Year sometime in February. The parades and cultural events for Lunar New Year are wonderful places to practice your Chinese, Vietnamese, or other Asian tongues.

Find out if there is a cultural organization in your area that represents the language you are learning. Call the nearest consulate or embassy of the country whose language you are learning and inquire about cultural centers in your area. The website of the embassy or consulate may even have links to cultural and language resources. Here's a website with a listing of all of the world's embassies: **www.embassyworld.com**

49. Find local language conversation groups

Once you become conversational in a language, you can add to your conversation partner experience by joining a language conversation group. In these groups, both native speakers and those learning the language meet to speak on a regular basis. This is a great way to meet natives and hear them speak to each other. I don't suggest joining one of these groups if you are still learning the basics of the language. Being around many fluent speakers who are speaking quickly may frustrate you. Wait until you at least achieve an intermediate to an advanced level in the language and can hold a conversation.

If you are in the United States, look for your local World Affairs Council (WAC) and see if there is an appropriate language group. The WAC organizes monthly language dinners for different languages: **www.worldaffairscouncils.org/**

Look for cultural or language groups in the Craigslist Community Section for your geographic area: **www.craigslist.org**

Meetup: This website is a place for people to start their own clubs and social groups related to whatever their interest area is. If you don't already have a Finnish Language Group in your area and you are studying that language, you can start your own group and see who in your area will join you. **www.meetup.com**

Contact the foreign language division of your local college or university. The department may have a list of resources for people looking to practice languages. You may be able to join the university's French Club or other language club.

50. Switch languages with your friends

If you have friends who are learning the same language as you are, switch your conversations to your new language. It may seem weird at first or even funny, but it will add spice to your interactions. Write emails to each other in the new language. Use the dictionary to look up words you do not know. Avoid using your native tongue as much as possible unless there are technical terms or idioms for which you can't find a translation.

51. Blog in your new language

If you already keep an online diary or blog, you can add entries in your new language or open a completely new blog in which you will only write in the new language. You can meet new readers this way. For example, a Japanese male blogger writes a Japanese language blog about horror films and wants to build up his audience and connect with other bloggers who write about the same topic. The Japanese man has been studying Portuguese for several years, and writes and understands at an advanced level. By accident, he finds a popular Portuguese language blog from Brazil that is focused on the same horror films that he likes. He decided to post his new blogs in both Japanese and Portuguese and increases his readership and has the opportunity to interact with horror film enthusiasts in Portuguese as well as Japanese.

The website **www.livejournal.com** has blogging sites in different languages. For example, you can blog in Russian and read other Russian language bloggers in your geographic area or from around the world.

52. Create a social networking profile in different languages

Do you have a profile on MySpace, Facebook, Gather, Ning, Orkut, or other social networking sites? How about creating one in your new language? Or if you already have one, you can join groups related to your language groups, interests, and background. Facebook has groups for people who attended French lycées (high schools), for those studying Swahili, and many other language or culture-centered groups. You can meet people with similar interests who either speak the language you are learning or are studying it just like you are.

If you are learning Portuguese or Hindi, consider joining Orkut. It's a social networking site that is very popular in Brazil and India.

Facebook **www.facebook.com**
Gather **www.gather.com**
MySpace **www.myspace.com**
My Space has a group just for people who like to study foreign languages **http://groups.myspace.com/languages**
Orkut: **www.orkut.com**

53. Join an Internet group in your new language

Maybe you don't fancy a public profile, but you still want to interact with people who speak your new language. Or you would like to add to your social networking experiences. Join a Yahoo or Google language group for your target language. Both sites have groups for people interested in foreign languages. If you are interested in parachuting, look for a parachuting lovers group in your new language. You can search for language, ethnic, cultural, or regional groups.

Go to these websites and browse through the different categories or just enter a search term for your language or region of choice:
http://groups.yahoo.com
http://groups.google.com/groups/dir

54. Chat

Join a chat room in Norwegian, find chat groups in Indonesian. The list is endless. Practice your written language skills by chatting with people on the Internet. You may have to download a chat program to your computer. You can find chat groups by language and topic.

ICQ http://groups.icq.com/groups
Pal Talk Chat http://chat.paltalk.com

Section 8: Day to Day

Exercises to Ingrain the Language
into Your Brain and Daily Rhythms

If you were learning to play an instrument, your teacher would advise you to practice everyday. Language is a muscle that needs to be flexed regularly. By incorporating these small, but key exercises into your daily life, you will notice how much easier it will be to recall words and have them flow from your mouth.

55. Listen to language learning CDs

To reinforce the grammar lessons in your language book, listen to language CDs at home, in your car, on your CD or MP3 player, or while exercising. There are many brands of language learning CDs like Rosetta Stone. As you listen to vocabulary lessons and conversations repeated on your CDs, you will see that you are able to understand more and more. This doesn't mean you can acquire the French subjunctive tense just by washing your dishes and listening to the same subjunctive lesson all week long, but this audio format is a wonderful addition to studying grammar with a book.

www.rosettastone.com
Online guide to various language learning
software: **www.languageresourceonline.com**

56. Learn on the go

You are busy. You want to learn Chinese while driving to work, commuting by bus, or waiting at the doctor's office. It's possible.

Praxis Language Learning Networks have created mobile podcasts of language lessons for Chinese, French, Spanish, English, and Italian that you can listen to and interact with on an MP3 Player/iPod, mobile phone, in a customized workbook or CD, on TV, on the Internet, or through a learning service/API. A native speaker and language learner use a conversational style to lead daily lessons in grammar, conversation, social customs, real life situations, stories, anecdotes, humor, mnemonic devices, etc. Students can print out lessons and flash cards from the website. There are also opportunities for students to study together online.

Students can choose which topics they like best and customize their lessons. The introductory podcasts are free and subscriptions including lessons and learning materials range from $5-23 a month.

www.praxislanguage.com

57. Combine it all with video, film, music, & conversation!

Immersing yourself in your target language is the key strategy to becoming fluent. Combining media such as video, film, music, and conversation with practical exercises is exactly what this book intends to communicate. To streamline your efforts at creating immersion, why not use a website which does all this for you? Yabla has created a set of multimedia activities using native speakers and authentic materials from television, movies, and music. For example, you can watch a current music video with the lyrics in subtitles in both the target language and English. Either set can also be hidden. The audio can be slowed down or 'looped' for easier listening comprehension. When you feel confident in understanding the song or video, there is also a game to test your knowledge of the text! In addition, there are coordinating lesson plans and a flash card service. Demonstration activities are available for free and subscriptions start at around $8 a month.

www.LoMásTv.com Spanish For Adult Learners
www.spanish.Yabla.com Spanish For K-12 Students
www.french.Yabla.com French for All
www.english.Yabla.com English as a Second Language

58. Talk to yourself in the language

Yes, that's right! Talk to yourself. When your language buddy is not nearby, you can talk to yourself as you are doing your household chores or washing your car. When you are thinking aloud about what you have to do today, say it in your new language. The point is for you to get used to saying everyday things in your new language. The more you use the language, the easier it becomes.

59. Balance your checkbook by counting in your new language

Even though you may or may not prefer to have your bank account in another country's currency, you should get used to regularly counting in the language. Going from counting in Japanese yen to Indian rupees may give you a heart attack as you see your net worth suddenly shrink, but don't think of the currency when you are counting, just the numbers. Speak out the numbers in your bank register as you are calculating. Even immigrants who have lived in an adopted country for over 20 years often still count in their native tongue. It's more natural to count in one's native tongue. However, when you are abroad and someone tells you a phone number really quickly or a bank teller is quoting you money conversion rates, you need to grasp those numbers instantaneously and be able to do your mental math in their language.

60. Make your to-do list and calendar in the language

Learn the words for your day-to-day tasks in your target language and use them as you keep yourself organized. Not only will you expand your vocabulary daily, you will also be thinking in another tongue.

Once you begin thinking of dry cleaning, grocery shopping, hardware store purchases, stationary, cleaning supplies, sporting goods, electronic equipment, and other items in your new tongue, you will naturally be adding to your vocabulary every week.

You are bored in a work meeting and you want to write your grocery shopping list. But you don't want the person next to you to know that you are not doing your work or see how healthy or unhealthy your purchases are, write the list in the new language. You're less likely to get caught!

Personal Story

I learned this from a Taiwanese coworker who used to write her to-do list in Chinese when we were in boring work meetings. It looked like she was taking meeting notes. Then, I did the same thing in Russian.

61. Label items in your home and office with sticky notes, using the foreign language

Recognition of household words will come easy if you mark your belongings with little stickers or adhesive paper with the words in your target language. List everything in your home and office in your language. Translate all the words you know and then look up the words that you don't know. Get adhesive notes like Post-it Notes or small pieces of paper and write the words in the new language. If you are using small pieces of paper, use tape to stick the papers to the items. Label everything. Even if you have two brooms and five mirrors, label them all so that you will constantly see the words. Say the name of the object when you see it.

62. If you have a CD alarm clock, set your wake up music to a song or greeting in your new language

Start your day with a song or language CD. You may not be completely awake, but you'll train your mind to get used to the sound of the new language before you get busy with your day.

63. Get ring tones for your mobile phone in your new language

Download foreign language songs as ringtones to your phone. You can have different songs for the most common people who call you. This may seem silly, but the point is to envelop yourself in the new language as much as possible. The more you hear the music...

There are many websites selling ringtones, these are just a few:
www.ringtonejukebox.com
www.thumbplay.com
www.ringophone.com

64. Read newspapers

Although this book focuses on how to learn languages through audio formats, I do not at all discount the importance of the written word. I am a writer who loves reading and writing. You need to read as well as listen. Find newspapers or magazines in newsstands, public libraries, or online. Read the news as much as possible. Reading will help you understand the TV news broadcasts you are watching.

List of newspapers worldwide organized by country:
www.ipl.org/div/news

http://dir.yahoo.com/News_and_Media/ Newspapers/By_Region/Countries

www.google.com/Top/News/Newspapers/ Regional

65. Foreign news aggregators

If you use an online news aggregation service that collects RSS feeds from blog and news sites, you can program it to collect news in a particular language. When you select the language of choice, keep in mind that all of your menu items and prompts will be in that language.

www.google.com/reader
www.bloglines.com

66. Read the same news stories in different languages

Culture is an inherent part of language. Reading the news in a different language can reveal unique cultural perspectives on world events. Some websites like Newstin.com function like on-line aggregation services such as Google Reader or Bloglines. But instead of subscribing to different news sites and blogs, Newstin does the work for you and brings you the latest news in the languages you choose. The website also allows you to search the headlines for certain topics and will display news about them in your preferred languages. By reading the same news stories in different languages, you gain another opportunity to practice your skills as well as experience different points of view from other cultures.

www.newstin.com/us/top-stories

67. Bilingual books/Parallel text

Though bilingual books are not easy to find, some publishers print books in two languages. The style is called "parallel text" with the original text and translation side by side. Foreign language poetry is sometimes published in this format. Search for books with parallel text from your target language.

Linguality Book club sends out a French or Italian book with an extensive English glossary placed opposite every page of text. It comes with a free audio CD with a 30- to 45-minute conversation in French or Italian with the author. **www.linguality.com**

The Penguin Publishing Company has a "New Penguin Parallel Text" series of books of short stories in Spanish, Italian, French, and German with English translations. **www.penguin.com**

68. Be a child

Being a child at heart makes almost everything in life easier and more fun. If you have children, learn a new language along with them. Beware, they might learn much faster than you. Even if you're 60 years old, that doesn't mean you can't watch *Sesame Street* or *Plaza Sésamo* in Spanish. Your child may say the word "Sí" (Spanish for yes) before he or she learns the word "yes" in your new language!

Slangman Productions has created books and television shows that help children learn French, Spanish, Italian, Chinese, Hebrew, German, and Japanese through fairy tales. Kids start reading a fairy tale in English and then gradually more and more foreign words are inserted into the English text, making it easy for them to still understand the context of the multilingual sentences. Fun videos supplement the books. These videos will soon be on TV. The fairy tale books are also available from Japanese to English and Chinese to English.

Some children's books are written for children to learn a new language or are written in both languages.

Children: Sesame Street has programs in Arabic, Bangla, Chinese, Dutch, German, Hebrew, Russian, and Spanish:
www.sesameworkshop.org/aroundtheworld

These companies publish bilingual children's books:
www.multiculturalkids.com (Go under the books section and select bilingual.)
www.slangman.com
www.languagelizard.com

69. Change menus

If you have an iPod, mobile phone or other electronic device with menus available in various languages, change the menu to your new language. You will force yourself to use your new language all the time while maneuvering your technological toys.

Day to Day

Section 9: Create Your World Contest Tips and Stories

Extra Tips Written By
Readers Like You

From February to April 2009, Kaleidomundi ran an online contest allowing interested readers to read the draft versions of *Language is Music* and *Travel Happy, Budget Low* online. Readers were encouraged to contribute their best language learning and budget travel tips and stories to the *Create Your World* Books Contest.

Praxis Language, Travel Document Systems, Kaehler World Traveler, Le Travel Store, Calling Cards.com and Adventure Medical Kits sponsored the contest with prizes.

Here, you can read the contest winners' submissions.

Thank you to all those who participated!

 ## Day-to-Day Exercises to Ingrain the Language Into Your Brain and Daily Rhythm

70. I have been exposed to Spanish (in high school), German (in college), French (with a private tutor) and Italian (self-study). I am FAR from fluent in any of these languages, but I have traveled in Switzerland, France and Italy and was able to make myself understood and travel around by myself.

In studying French and Italian I found the Pimsleur cassette courses very valuable. The method there is to listen and repeat at a faster pace as you go along. There is no grammar or reading.

Gerald Comisar

www.pimsleur.com

 Miscellaneous

71. If you take your children to a foreign country, encourage them to speak the language. Before traveling in Mexico with my children, I taught my 9-year-old daughter a few Spanish words and phrases. Initially she was too shy to speak them. Finally, on a hot day at the archeological ruins in Tula, when she was extremely thirsty, I refused to buy her a drink. Instead I gave her the money and suggested a way to ask for what she wanted. Very reluctantly, she did so and returned with her favorite soda. That broke the ice and she was more relaxed about speaking Spanish. My four children are bilingual; thanks to extensive trips I took with them, travelling on native busses in Mexico and Guatemala. We spoke Spanish exclusively and found that people eagerly conversed with us because we were not the typical "Ugly American" travelers. During four trips, we traveled 16,000 miles—mostly to out-of-the way places including archeological ruins in jungles, and an isolated volcano. One son met future pen pals on those trips and now, 38 years later, is still in touch with them. When my son's twin daughters were born, he wanted them to become fluent in Spanish so he spoke to them only in that language. His wife learned along with the kids.

The girls are in middle school now and excel in Spanish. What's even more satisfying is that they now correspond in Spanish with the children of my son's original Mexican pen pals.

Anita Goldwasser

72. Listen to books in other languages
I am a native French speaker. While driving roundtrip from Switzerland to Sweden, I listened to the Swedish-language audiobook version of *The Da Vinci Code* by Dan Brown. It was perfect to learn and listen to the sound of the language. I could concentrate on just listening to the book and I had a great story to listen to. I never found driving for so many hours to be so pleasant. The speakers in audio books are always articulating well.

Read the book in the new language at the same time as you are listening to the audio book, it will have the same effect as having a movie with subtitles in the new language.

Marc-Aurèle Brothier

73. Flex those language muscles!
Keep what you have learned with regular practice. When I moved back from Sweden to Switzerland, I didn't want to forget my Swedish. Now, I'm reading Swedish books, watching Swedish news, and listening to Swedish radio. It's like a sport, if you stop training you will lose what you've gained!

Marc-Aurèle Brothier

74. Keep your brain in action
My translator friend suggested that multilingual people should alternate the languages of the books they are reading. Switch as much as possible! The more you go from one language to another, the more adept your mind is at processing the languages.

Marc-Aurèle Brothier

75. Multilingual news
If you have trouble reading or watching the news in your target language, read or watch the news in the morning in your language and then read or watch the evening news in your target language. You will be familiar with the content from the morning news and it will be easier to understand the news in your new language. You will also see what developments have occurred throughout the day.

When I arrived in New York, I used to buy the Daily News newspaper (in English) before getting on the subway as well as the local Russian newspaper, Novoie Russkoie Slovo. When I had time, I also bought Pravda or Izvestia, the Soviet newspapers. On the way to work, I would read the news in English and on the way home, I read the news in Russian covering the same topics I had read about in the morning in English. Since I had already read the news in English, it was easier for me to understand the vocabulary and topics. I could easily understand new words because I understood their context.

I improved my vocabulary every day and I learned the point of view of the Russian community in the US from the local papers and the official position of the Soviet government from the Soviet papers.

Miguel Vargas-Caba

76. Alphabet soup

If you are learning a language with a different alphabet, like the Cyrillic alphabet, write out common words or the lyrics of a song from your own language in that new alphabet. This way you are forcing yourself to use the new alphabet for words you already know.

Miguel Vargas-Caba

 Personal Story:
What does it mean to be a global citizen?
Anita Goldwasser

My life changed after my sons and I had our first adventure in Mexico. They wanted to collect insects in the jungle so we left Tijuana by bus bound for the jungle town of San Blas, Nayarit.

To reach our destination, we traveled on a second class bus with broken windows. As rain splashed onto my clothing, men with machetes boarded the bus (They worked at a pineapple plantation). We passed scenes that reminded me of photos in the National Geographic Magazine showing native women washing clothing in streams. In San Blas, chickens and mangy dogs wandered in and out of the tiny bus station. I loved it. This was the "real Mexico."

We made four additional trips, traveling 16,000 miles in Mexico and Guatemala – immersing ourselves in the life of both countries and speaking Spanish all the time. What was the result? I quit working in a lab and became a freelance writer and photographer, selling articles based on our experiences. *My children learned first-hand about life in both countries and are now bilingual. One son subsequently lived in Mexico and went to school there for a year.*

I was 44 years old when I made the first trip -- and had forgotten much of my high school Spanish. Luckily, I worked in a food processing plant alongside Mexican-Americans and they introduced me to Mexican Spanish. They chuckled at the Castilian Spanish I had learned in New York years earlier.

We've traveled on busses with animals as fellow passengers, hitchhiked in the wilderness, climbed pyramids at archeological sites, and marveled at the genius of the early civilizations in both countries. At Tikal, our small plane barely cleared the trees when it landed in the jungle.

In Oaxaca, my younger son purchased fajas at an Indian market and exchanged addresses with the young girl selling them. They became pen pals. And on another trip to Oaxaca, we sought out her family. One taxi driver refused to take us, claiming that the neighborhood was too dangerous. Another driver took us but couldn't find the house. Finally and old woman tending goats overheard my son and said, "Wait while I tie my goats to a tree and I'll show you where the family lives." She did. I spent the most memorable evening in their humble one-room home, built by the father. We conversed entirely in Spanish. Later the pen pal took us to a church meeting. A 15-year-old boy on my left practiced speaking English with me. On my right, a woman in her native costume nursed her baby. I was thrilled to experience the "Old" and "New" in Mexico simultaneously.
The following year, I stayed at the home of a different pen pal in Mexico City's worst slum. Being able to speak Spanish allowed me to

fully experience Mexico and communicate with the people.

My grandchildren now correspond in Spanish with the children of my son's original pen pals. Thus, two generations remain linked.

About the Author

My multilingual skills and bulging passport filled with stamps from exotic places like Tajikistan and Cambodia have provided many international adventures.

I am a world traveler and polyglot whose goal is to empower people to be global citizens who are knowledgeable about world events and are confident international travelers and communicators. I have studied ten languages (English, Russian, French, Spanish, Italian, Portuguese, Serbo-Croatian, Hebrew, Arabic, and Hungarian) and speak seven of them. (Only vestiges of Hungarian, Hebrew, and Arabic remain in my memory.) Via my trajectory through the languages I speak, the nine countries I have lived in, and the 50 nations I have visited, I have become a citizen of the world. After teaching English in Argentina, Bosnia, and the United States, I realized how to make foreign language learning fun and easy through listening exercises and music.

My wanderlust started at an early age, fueling my world travels. While living, studying or working abroad, I traveled extensively in the regions where I was located. Throughout my life, I found that each time I learned a new language, I added new worlds to my existence. These are some highlights of my world trajectory as related to my language skills:

My family immigrated to the United States from the Soviet Union when I was three years old. At a young age, I began to feel that I had two different worlds as my Russian language home life dramatically contrasted with my English speaking existence. We spent two years in St. Louis, Missouri and then moved to Silicon Valley, California. When I was 11, I began to study both Hebrew and French. At 15, I was a foreign exchange student in Pornichet, France. Though I had to cut short my French stay after two months because I lived with a dysfunctional French family, I did become fluent in French and had the opportunity to start learning Spanish. After the dramatic French séjour, I went to the other side of the Atlantic to a boarding school near Boston, Massachusetts. The cold of New England turned me back home to study at the University of California at Berkeley, where I studied Political Economy, continued my Spanish education, and picked up Italian. Curious to learn about life in another former Communist country besides the Soviet Union, I completed my last semester abroad in Budapest, Hungary, where I learned basic Hungarian.

After graduating with honors from the University of California at Berkeley, I knew that I either wanted to work as a journalist or in international development. Choosing the easier route, I worked for the United States Department of Commerce helping Silicon Valley companies export. To add spice to my banal office worker life, I taught myself Portuguese. Unable to completely ignore my passion for writing, I combined both international work and journalism while turning my life upside down to live at the end of the world in Buenos Aires, Argentina in 1999. Under the auspices of a Rotary Ambassadorial Scholarship, I studied at the Universidad de Buenos Aires, interned in the Commercial Section of the United States Embassy, edited and wrote for the English language daily, the *Buenos Aires Herald*, and taught English. Shortly after returning to California from South America, I realized that my impulse to travel was as strong as ever. I left for Bosnia, where I designed economic development projects in war-torn areas for the International Rescue Committee and Mercy Corps. Being a native Slavic language speaker helped me learn Serbo-Croatian in Sarajevo.

Though I thoroughly appreciated living in Bosnia, I was ready to go back to sunny California in late 2001, but I couldn't live without some cross-cultural experience. For two years, I worked as a substitute teacher and employed my Spanish language skills to research the role of religion in the lives of Mexican and Salvadoran immigrants for a Pew Trust research project at the University of San Francisco. To augment my globetrotting experiences, I observed elections in Armenia, Tajikistan, and Ukraine for the US State Department and the Organization for Security and Cooperation in Europe Inspired by my Middle Eastern travels, I briefly studied Arabic.

Savoring the culinary side of being an international gourmet, I used my Italian language skills to market Italian wines in San Francisco and promoted the Slow Food Movement. When I became allergic to grapes and the main ingredients to Italian cuisine, I realized I had abandoned my passion: writing. In September 2005, I quit the world of wining and dining and dedicated myself to writing my memoir, *One-Eyed Princess in Babel: Seeing the World With My Ears*.

I live in Cupertino, California.

For more information about Susanna's work, please visit: **www.createyourworldbooks.com**

Other Titles by Susanna Zaraysky

Travel Happy, Budget Low: Over 200 Money Saving Tips to See The World
(Part of the *Create Your World* book series)

Do you want to see the world, but your bank account isn't ready for a four star, or even three-star hotel?

You can do it. Allow yourself the luxury of seeing the world!

In 17 years, I've traveled to over 50 countries. People always marvel at how I travel so widely on a limited budget. Over 200 tips and 161 website resources cover the topics of frequent flyer mile tricks, health/safety, expenditures, packing, passports/visas, preparation, customs and more. Included are some comic and bizarre anecdotes from my travels.

Travel Happy, Budget Low is a primer on how to travel well and be frugal anywhere in the world. Other travel books are location specific.

The most costly elements of travel are transportation, lodging and food. *Travel Happy, Budget Low* informs you how to travel economically in planes, trains, and buses, how to find inexpensive meals, and how to book inexpensive hotel rooms or stay for free with locals.

Budget travel does not mean you will spend weeks on rickety old buses with no ventilation or spend the night in run-down hostels. You don't have to sleep in bus stations. (I've only done it once!)

You will realize that you too can see Paris, The Great Wall of China, the Vienna Opera, and other great sites without breaking the bank.

Enrich yourself culturally without being rich!

One-Eyed Princess in Babel: Seeing the world with my ears
(To be published in 2011)

This is my memoir about how I discovered my global identity via my linguistic trajectory through a modern day Tower of Babel.

At the age of 29, I found out that my world was flat. Unlike 95% of the population, I had been using only one eye at a time and saw in two dimensions. My world turned on its heels. I had always been ashamed of my eyes. In the Soviet Union, I had to go to a day care for retarded children because I was cross-eyed. The discovery about my limited vision led me to unravel a mystery: my gift for languages. I spoke Russian, English, French, Spanish, Italian, Portuguese, and Serbo-Croatian and had studied Hebrew, Hungarian, and Arabic. I never knew why I was so gifted with languages until I realized that my excellent communication skills created the multidimensional world that I couldn't see. Metaphorically speaking, I saw with my ears.

Languages were the lenses through which I saw the world. Each chapter traces how I acted and thought differently in each tongue.

Disoriented by my lack of cultural identity, I lived the life of a global nomad. Via a series of extraordinary events, my Mom broke free from the Iron Curtain by contacting long lost American relatives who helped us escape the repressive Soviet Union. When I came to the U.S. as a child, I faced a dual battle of being labeled "red" and feeling defective for being cross-eyed. Neither American nor Russian culture felt like "home" to me. During my soul-searching quest, I studied many languages and traveled in 50 countries. Whether listening to the melancholic prosody and antagonism of Slavic languages or the whispering and nagging sounds of French or the fun and coquettish charm of Spanish and Italian, my character changed depending on the sounds and rhythm of the language I was utilizing.

I was a linguistic chameleon. As a result, I didn't feel attached to any one culture or language, and this lack of identity caused me great anxiety in spite of being one of the few people able to communicate across language borders in my metaphorical Tower of Babel. Overwhelmed with being able to hear and understand many sounds and languages simultaneously, I had trouble finding my own inner voice and knowing who I was. Eventually, I realized that my lack of roots, or multi-rootedness, actually created my identity. My dysfunctional eyes gave me the ability to be a global citizen.

Index

LaVergne, TN USA
24 June 2010
187283LV00004B/10/P